As We Soar

As We Soar

Sandra Leon-Gonzalez

empoweredtoself@gmail.com

Copyright © 2025 Sandra Leon-Gonzalez
Printed in the United States of America
First Edition

ISBN 979-8-218-88792-6

First Printing, 2025

This book is dedicated to the reader,
with gratitude.

Contents

The Focus of Love

Introduction:
A Tapestry of Love, Light, Truth, and Awareness

Poetry is more than words—it is the heartbeat of the soul, the quiet revelation of beauty in all its forms. This collection is a journey, woven with verses that embrace love as both refuge and revolution, light as a guide through darkness, truth as the foundation upon which we stand, and awareness as the lens through which we see more deeply.

Each poem is a reflection, an invitation to pause and listen—to the whispers of history, the echoes of resilience, and the quiet strength of human connection. Love is not merely sentiment; it is a force that transforms. Light does not merely illuminate; it reveals. Truth does not merely stand; it endures. And awareness is not merely understanding; it awakens.

As you turn these pages, may you find yourself immersed in words that uplift and challenge, that comfort and ignite, that honor the past while illuminating the present. This book is not just poetry— it is a call to remember, to feel, and to rise.

Welcome to this journey. Let's begin.

As We Soar

Ancestral Strength

Whispers of My Ancestors

We walked through fire
yet here we stand
rooted deep in this promised land.
Chains could bind
but not erase;
the fire in our souls reflects light in our face.

We sang through sorrow
and danced through pain.
We were bent, not broken
standing tall again.
The winds may howl,
the storms will rise,
but hope still glows in weary eyes.

Children of tomorrow
hear our calls;
we are the dreams
still standing tall.
Lift your voices, let justice ring
for freedom is the song
we will always sing.
Our hands once built
our backs once bore
our strength remains forevermore.
So rise with courage
and walk with Grace;
the future will bloom
in your embrace.

RESPECT
EXISTENCE
ANTIFA
INTERNATIONAL
OR EXPECT
RESISTANCE

Still We Stand

Through blood, sweat, and pain,
through the whips and chains,
they have tried to silence,
tried to drain.

Yet our roots run deep
with echoes loud,
we're a people unbowed;
we are forever proud.

We bore the weight,
the scars and cries.
We rose like the phoenix
with unshaken eyes.

From cotton fields
to city streets,
we build, we dream
we take our seats.

They wrote us out to dim our names,
but history burns an endless flame,
though every storm and every tear,
we prove again: We're still here.

We're not just surviving
we're standing tall
we're breaking chains
to defy it all.

Through generations of grit,
we are bold and free.
We will carve our place,
our legacy.

Through sorrow's tide,
through hope's embrace,
Black hands still lift
to light each space.

The past is heavy,
the struggles long,
yet in our veins,
the song is strong.

Still we fight, still we rise,
still our fire fills the skies;
not forgotten, never erased,
we are here, claiming our place.

A New Definition

I am rewriting my own narrative
shaking off the one force on me.
I am the author of my own story
showing true light for all to see.

My ancestral eyes have seen kingdoms
with treasures beyond any dream.
You cannot lie to history
no matter how real it's made to seem.

My existence is so much bigger
than any story concocted for me,
since my dreams are locked in my vision
and I'm the only one holding the key.

Nothing you do can hold me hostage,
I was created to be free!
There is nothing that can hold me
since I'm created just to be.

Can you see the aura around me?
It's a glow of magnificent lights.
My commitment to each moment
is to elevate and reach new heights.

Women's
Rights
Are
Human
Rights
NOT YOUR
BODY
NOT YOUR
CHOICE
healthcare
FAT
GOV'T
SOME
WHO HAD
AN ABORTION

Making A Change

Leaning into the silence of knowing
where I am always free
from all restraint of society
that has been placed on me.

My feminine wilds
I dare to show
letting the world know
women are here to grow.

Do you still think
you can muffle our voices
in making decisions
to eliminate our choices?

Making laws about our ovaries
without the right to make a plea
yet you never gave a thought
about what's right for me.

You've designed medical treatments
base on male physiology
without the necessary research
to address our femininity.

You're asking us to trust you
then make decisions considerate of all
if it's only for your agenda
you have no right to make that call.

WOMEN'S RIGHTS
MY BODY MY CHOICE

We have come too far in fighting
to addressing women's needs
we are taking our seats at the table
becoming part of those who lead.

The universe will hold us
as we celebrate with Divinity
as we evolved in our creation
glowing in unity.

My Vision Quest

As I walked in
nature's Eden,
my ancestors
communed with me.

I had so many questions
and they had
all the answers
for me.

When asked about
my struggles,
they made it clear
so that I could see

that if it wasn't
for all life brought me
would I be forged into
the warrior you now see.

Those lessons came
with fixed endorsement
promoting strength and vigor
for my growth and prosperity.

Deal With
GRL
PWR

Power Realized

In order to be galvanized
we must be organized
to identify the danger
that lurks beneath the lies.

The division is no accident;
it is a defined precedent
to keep us distracted
while our rights become less relevant.

Spaghetti gets thrown on the wall
to see what sticks and what falls
while the volume becomes chaos
to distract and confuse us all.

Let's focus on the business to choose
and be united or we will lose
with clarity to see the truth
but in the noise, we are confused.

Don't let the distraction into your ear
that agenda is just to promote fear
there is nothing that we lack—
we are powerful, let that be clear.

IGNORANCE
OF THE
PRIVILEGED
IS
DEADLY
TO THE
OPPRESSED

BLACK LIVES MATTER!

Driven

My strides have become
more purposeful
as I walk in dignity.
rejecting all the lies.

Using the footsteps
of my ancestors
their strength of struggles
are guiding me to the light.

Nat Turner was killed
for waging a revolution,
but freedom is deserved
no matter what the cost.

The bravery of Harriet Tubman
leading the Underground Railroad
pushes me forward
in this life I call my own.

Rosa Parks stayed in her seat
so that I am able to stand
to echo the sentiments of others
still being abused in this land.

Sojourner highlighted
the intersection of race and gender—
"Ain't I a woman?"
expounded on her Truth.

I AM
BLACK
HISTORY

Ruby showed grit
as she Bridges the divide
I will channel her courage
exposing all lies.

Martin's dream brought hope
envisioning unity and peace;
let's stand together
and see that it's revealed.

No need to regurgitate stories
history knows the Truth
symbolism is not substance
and lies cannot replace Facts.

The Knight Within

Through shadows deep,
through storm-torn skies,
my spirit reborn, again I rise.

No distant hero,
no waiting plea,
the blade of fate, belongs to me.

Each fall, each wound,
each whispered doubt,
I forged my strength, I cast them out.

No savior's call,
no borrowed light,
I stand alone, my armor bright.

The battle rages,
the echoes cry,
yet in my heart, the stars reply.

For every loss,
for every tear,
I wield my will, I banish fear.

Not once, not twice,
but evermore,
I claim my place, I guard my core.

A knight, a queen,
a force unbowed,
I rise again, my fate is proud.

Born To Be

I am a warrior,
battle-ready from my birth.
After my gender revealed
gifted my shield and armor
to fight to secure my place on Earth.

I'm an Amazonian,
oh yes, I am a queen.
I am determined
and will slay
those who try to conquer me.

Don't make rules for me.
I'm boundless and I'm free.
I am the mother of this earth you see;
so how can any man
place claims on me?

Your politic is slander
just an effort to shackle me;
what you see as weakness
I will show you
it's strength and power in me.

I wear my scars like badges
of the battles
you've put me through,
and I will never stop fighting
until I get what's due.

Your gender polls confine me,
but I'm determined
to make sure they're broken down
to see a new beginning
where equality reigns all around.

And when that day is upon us—
it's destined,
you will see—
I'll raise my hands and shout
forever victory.

Let Freedom Ring

History Will Speak

The story of the barn
is still not fully told
of how Emmett Till's body
was left lifeless and cold.

The silence of untold stories
will not render them dead
there will always be a reckoning
and it will all be said.

That's a long time ago
is the excuse being used
yet for history to be known
the telling is the fuse.

Black parents still wail
for the lives of their sons
while others pretend
that no more can be done.

Evolution cannot be stifled
no matter the muzzles held on
your reign will be temporary
and one day you'll be gone.

The Win

What to me is your
celebration of liberty,
when in fact it was never
afforded to me?

What to me is innocent
until proven guilty,
when people like me
are sentenced unjustly?

What to me is your
Independence Day,
when at its inception
my people were not free?

What to me
is being labeled violent,
when you owned brutality
of lynching by decree?

What to me is rising
seems to elevate your fear,
the zero-sum is then launched
and terror is now near.

What to me is fighting
for my freedom,
while for supremacy
you make laws to limit me.

THE
LIGHT
OF
TRUTH

What for me is
non-violent protest,
to those using violence
in holding necks under knees.

What to me is light
shining brightly so all can see,
hate as your motivator
and the truth will come to be.

What to me is hope
in the beauty to be seen,
because evil never wins
no matter how it seems.

Denk
TRUTH
cubeoftruth.com

Eyes Wide Closed

The fire is out
under the melting pot
since fear-based hate
has been placed on spot.

The chants of negativity
now fill the air
and all this ugliness
will cause despair.

In touting hate's rhetoric
and destroying unity built
we are wrapping ourselves
in a disastrous quilt.

May hope ride in
and save us all
before this downturn
causes our fall.

With open hearts
let's dare to see
the oneness in truth
and how beautiful we can be.

Lost

Tears will fall
as evil thrives;
the fault will be
giving in to lies.

You closed your eyes
and bowed to fears;
but in our midst
we lose our cares.

Visions lost
become unseen;
as the weight of struggles
has made us mean.

Denial of facts
doesn't make them less real;
you've lost yourself
to a fate now sealed.

We are always able
to return to the light;
and then refocus
on a future that's bright.

DO NOT
ENTER
WRONG
WAY

Lost in the Rhetoric

Sticks and stones
they're all being thrown
just like the lies
that are now told.
Departing from truth,
the brutes now rule
as they bully their way
with enough falsehood
that it should be a crime.

It's all about the power
distorted politic brings
as religion is contorted
making innocence a sin.
Dignity and ethics
now on hiatus
while unscrupulous players
highlight their agendas
and dominate our news.

Let's take a step back
to when decency reigned.
Let's hold truth to the light
changing our course trajectory
since the path now presented
is a minefield of ugly hate.
We are better than these moments.
In truth and freedom there is greatness
and that power is ours to perceive.

Dont lie

The Reveal

Hypocrisy and gaslighting
are now holding hands,
the two joined together
is an unholy band.

Yellow journalism and propaganda
are dominating the news,
while freedom is banned
stifling our views.

How did we get here,
this decent into Hell,
allowing fear to guide us
ringing its victory bell?

Power and greed,
corruption and lies,
are now being accepted
as if they're a prize.

Hate has been put on display
like an ornament on a shelf,
but in showing this to others
you are reflecting yourself.

Have we learned nothing
from past tyrant's regime,
as oppression keeps mounting
making suffering a theme?

HSTORY

Your names will be revealed
and the truth will come out;
history will record
what you are all about.

Reflection of disdain
will be your historic reward
and lessons will be taught
to prevent this discord.

The Turning Point

In battles waged
let there be no war;
the cost of that
will go too far.

Let's use the mind
and start with grit;
we are so much stronger
when we use our wits.

Stop allowing fear
to push us to harm;
instead allow love
to make us calm.

A diplomatic route
can see us through;
instead of seeking power
with selfish brutes.

In finding peace
humanity wins;
without striking a blow
to anyone's chin.

The world can seek
to thrive as one;
and relinquish the madness
that baseless lies spun.

Liberty
&
Justice
for
ALL!

I See You

Dr. King's dream was just the start.
Now it's time for us to do our part,
moving forward in love and unity
seeing the oneness of humanity.

The pandemic lockdown bought time to reflect,
to see the oppression that sits on our neck.
Seeing George Floyd killed ignited a spark
and started a fire in all of our hearts.

Keep the dream intact to be enforced.
Don't let the haters throw us off our course.
Let us pull together hearing freedom's cries,
dispelling the rhetoric and all of the lies.

The pushing of stories of zero-sum
that for one to win, it's at the expense of some.
We must dispel the regurgitation of that myth
to realize the dream by showing pure grit.

The test of our humanity now in full view
to the mountain top we go in multiple hues,
shedding all prejudice like old worn-out shoes;
freedom has won and that is good news.

We Did the Work

With all that I've accomplished,
I refuse to have it taken from me.
With all my ancestral struggles
the dream is mine to perceive.

Nothing I have was ever given
without a detrimental cost to me.
This journey has always been tireless,
yet in the distance there is light I see.

I am determined to push forward
with the awareness that beckons.
I'll show the world my grit with fervor
navigating traps that are set for me.

I'm done with the empty promises
since your deceptions taught me well,
to ignore valueless comments
and fight for the truth I want to tell.

What trickery do you think you can sell me?
Freedom Road is being built without fear.
There is nothing you can do to stop it,
this life is mine to breathe in, just like air.

The Essence of Time

Tick-tock
I'm watching my clock
and I have no time for that.
No time for petty squabbles
or conversations lacking truth.
No time for fabricated stories
and gossiping with fools.
No time for baseless excuses
for why my story is left untold.
No time for the whitewashed agenda
as you watch racism take hold.
No time for your hands on my ovaries
dictating when I will give birth.
No time for your hypocrisy
when your morality is in the dirt.
No time for you to speak on safety
while refusing to make gun laws.
No time for you to use religion
as the basis for the ills you do.
No time for your concessions
all you've done will come back to you.
Your time is up!

Power Is Internal

Journey to Self

As the dawn awaits
for all who will open their eyes,
we awake with expectations
of what we choose to believe
which can bring us disappointments
since none of it is real.

We construct infinite stories
about others and ourselves,
our minds then tend to wonder
creating fears derive from lack,
divisions become cemented
and the sadness never stops.

Dawn has no story,
Divinity unfolds the path.
It's all laid out before you.
Listen to the silence beneath the chat
to help you fuel your journey
as your patience is now intact.

Like nature in its stillness
we can then be guided back
to the pathway of our purpose
holding truth as a guiding light,
and in the fullness of these moments
our oneness is now resumed.

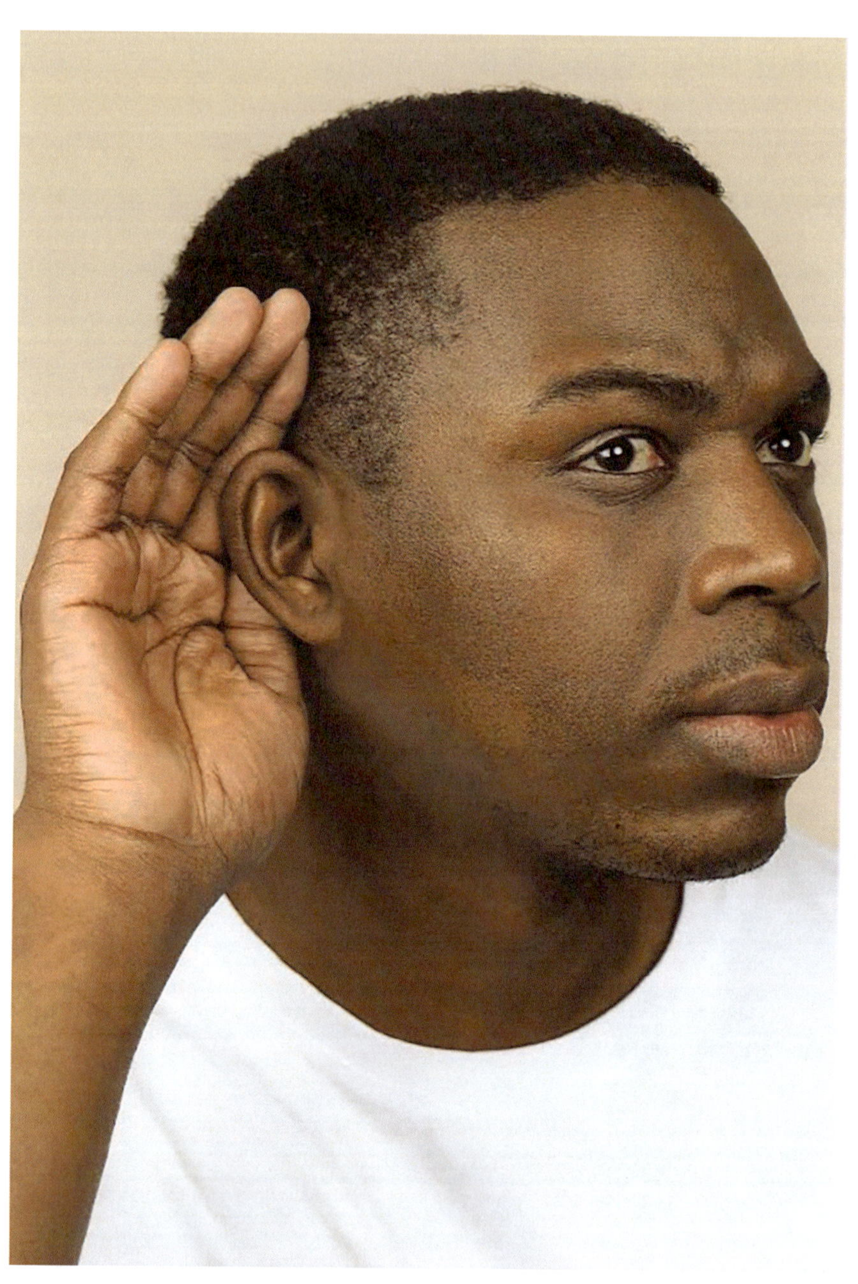

Just Listen

In the silence of my mind
I am set free.
I am in a beautiful place
where I am one with Divinity.

As the silence speaks
true knowing will come,
and in that moment
Thy will be done.

No words are needed
it's all understood,
everything life brings you
is all to your good.

Let go and be guided,
your path is in view.
Hold truth in acceptance
it's all up to you.

Your purpose now in focus,
cemented as your creed,
growth to infinity,
you have all that you need.

Growth to Infinity

You thought that you could break me
by creating a narrative of lack.
You just didn't see it coming
when in turn I bounced right back.

You thought that you could bend me
by restricting information taught.
But in my inherent curiosity
true knowledge was then brought.

You thought you could control me
by trying to diminish my very worth,
but in turning my focus inward
I realized it was stitched in at birth.

You thought in placing restrictions
you would criminalize my very dream,
but you were short-sighted in your vision:
I created a workaround for your scheme.

You thought you could hold me down
with the weight from your knee,
but my growth has been much stronger
and I have obliterated your superiority dream.

Peace Wins

When turmoil settles in
with chaos and fear in the front row,
you can choose how to be
and not attend the show.

It is all just a distraction
to lure you from the truth,
and when you lose your focus
you've bitten the forbidden fruit.

Confusion can settle in
as fear entwines your mind,
and develop negative spins
that makes you so unkind.

Identify the hold,
you are stronger than you think!
Look past the noise
and sever this hateful link,

As you regain your full control
the truth will then unfold,
to now regain the peace
that fear almost stole.

A Bold Realization

There was a time when I did not see
the beautiful light that lived in me.
There was a time when I did not know
that this inner light was there to glow.

There was a time when I could not feel
how worthy I am and how to embrace that zeal.
There was a time when I questioned that worth
but then realized I got it at birth.

There was a time when I did not embrace my power
instead, fear would take hold and I would cower.
But when my power was allowed to be viewed
fear was discarded and now I'm renewed.

There was a time that I did not know love
but I open my heart and it pour in from above.
Love is the thing that transcends all other
leaving you free with no time to bother.

There was a time when nothing was clear
now with my gifts I've left doubts in the rear.
There was a time when I questioned if I would succeed,
but now I know I have all that I need.

Empowered

I wield the power
I was born with.
My worthiness
is etched in my veins.

There is no separation
from my dignity.
If you tried, it would be
to your own pain.

My eyes recognize
all that is beautiful
since beauty
is an intricate part of me.

My existence
is destined for greatness.
It's the truth
of my very being.

The stories you tell
can't sway me
when I'm confident
in all I conceive.

The light I shine
has no dimmer.
It's like lightning
in my bloodstream.

So here I am showing up
in full acceptance
because who I am
is all up to me.

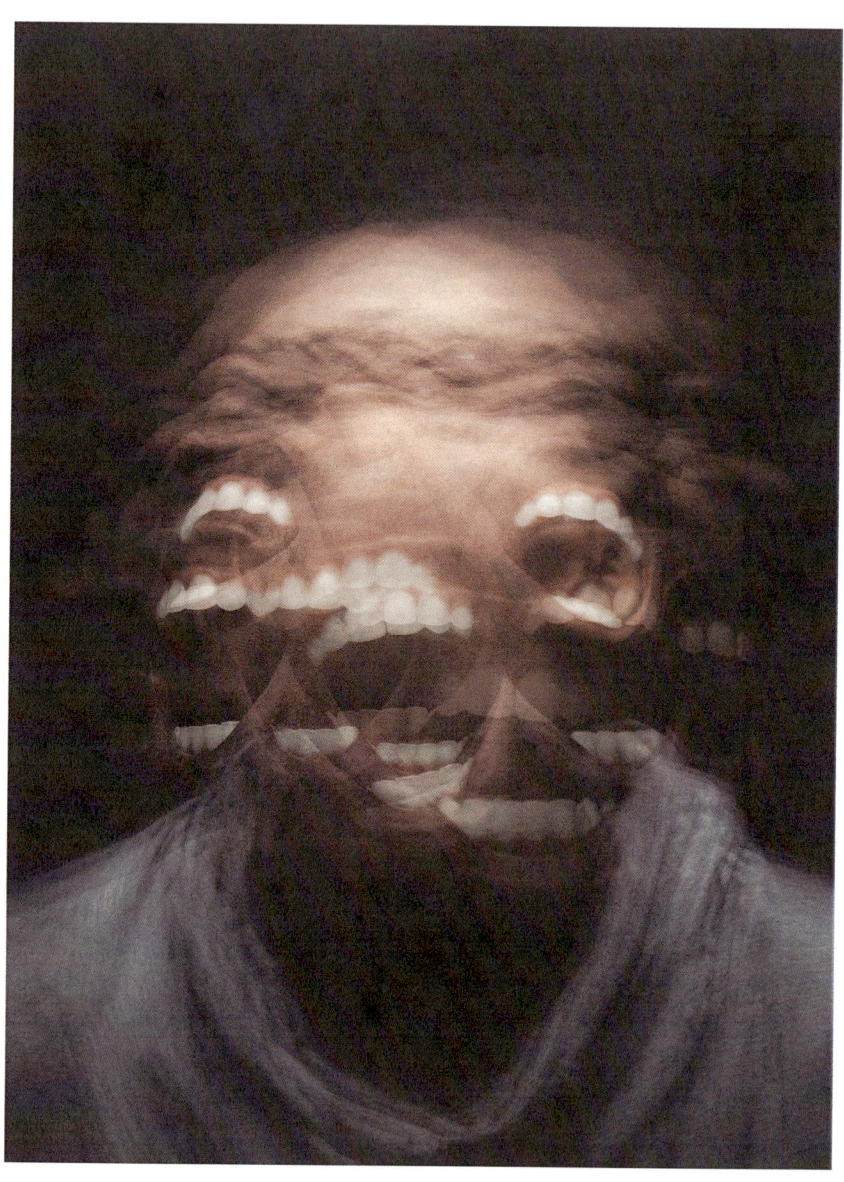

Self-Control

Breath is hastened
as fingers tap
eyes now glaring
as lips are pursed
not holding anger back.

The wait is draining
growing more furious still
as the heart starts pounding
and emotions heightened
as blame replaces will.

The feeling is maddening
as nostrils flare
take a breath regain control
you are the author
of how this story is told.

Your emotions are heightened
but you know what to do:
close your eyes and look inwards,
the answers lie within you.
Losing control is never a win.

Channel your breath calmly
your thoughts will then settle in
as it finds the right solution
and make a clear decision
to solve the problem you're in.

Now as anger leaves you
and rational thoughts
begin to flow,
you'll find it much easier
to learn as you grow.

On This Path

I celebrate me
for my resiliency,
for creating
a space of peace
where I can
revel in my authenticity,
knowing that my worth
was given at birth
and it cannot
be ripped from me.
Not by words or deeds,
I am grounded
in the truth of my strength.
There is no force
that can limit me.

I rejoice for who
I'm becoming
because I am
the joy that I seek.
I am the love
that has been given
and the one I now receive.
These are chapters
that are yet unwritten.
The full story
is not yet revealed
but I'm bold enough to
take this journey
so you can see
the best of me.

Save Your Judgement

I'm a masterpiece in view
beautifully scarred
and loving every one.
They teach me to be
grateful for battles
I have won.
These scars I wear
although now healed
were once-open wounds
that caused me much grief.

They're my shields of honor,
I wear them all with pride.
Shame has been banished:
I own and love them all
without any blame.
Divinity brought them to me
to strengthen my focus
in showing me all I can be.
I don't have to hide them;
They're mine to reveal.

Covered or naked,
I am born just to be.
This life is a treasure
that I hold in esteem.
No hidden agendas,
just living my truth.
I'm a warrior emboldened,
beautiful and flawed,
living in each moment
but knowing when to pause.

Shining

I'm like a star
in Orion's Belt
with a glow
everyone can see.

I was created
with this brightness
since the light
is forged in me.

May you know
truth in my actions
because the truth
is all I can be.

To forge a beautiful
and lasting connection
not just for you
in fact it's for me.

My existence
is but a catalyst
to propel me
to shine infinitely.

The Focus of Love

New Connections

In the midst of those
once not meant for me,
I can still hold my own.

In those moments,
no shrinking to
hide the truth of me.

I can find comradery
in the exploration of fact
leading to new insights.

The newest of perceptions
can open doors
that were once sealed.

Choosing openness to connect
can make new friends
of supposed enemies.

In the light of truth
our connections thrive
and keeps the beauty of hope alive.

The Medicine For Life

I've loved before
and I'll love again,
no matter the release,
the means or the end.

Loving in any form
brings light to your day.
It embraces dark clouds
to work through the pain.

In the throes of all tears
when your head is in a spin,
love harnesses strength
from deep within.

Even when there is loss
and you're falling apart,
memories act as love's thread
in mending your heart.

So hold on to love
in all that you do,
it's the medicine that fixes
all you go through.

Heart Held

Tempest moon in lifted sky,
my body swoons before your eyes.
I see your face and know your gaze
as you hold me close in warm embrace.

The daylight now in blazing sun
for now our day has just begun.
The heat there now is tempered down
as we lay our bodies on the ground.

Oh tell me now where love begins.
It feels like fire beneath our skin
as we hold our gaze in loving care
restraining thoughts of all we dare.

How can it be we feel so much
with tenderness always in a rush?
With open eyes we can still dream
with muffled passion, we dare not scream.

I'm here for you and you for me.
Our love transcends eternity.
I breathe you in like air in my lungs
as our heart songs beat just like a drum.

The Comfort of Love

Two hearts now linked
to beat as one
with love so deep
burning hotter than the sun.

Our roots are fused
as we nourish our growth.
Our hearts rejoice
with all love's oath.

We are not just a chance
that came to be,
our union was destined
as everyone can see.

As we glow in our romance,
with every moment well-spent,
never seeing time past,
or caring where it went.

Like separated souls
that connected anew,
now we're cemented
fitting as if with glue.

The Power of Love

May we always see
the glow of love in each other's eyes.
May we always know
the answers to love's questions
without ever asking why.

May each passing moment
push us further into bliss.
May our kisses feel like sunshine
with rays lingering on our lips
like a favorite song you want to sing.

May we know how to love each other
because we love ourselves.
May we feel the joy of having
love putting us under a spell
and hoping it never ends.

May we show up for each other
seeing wounds that need to mend.
May we be grateful for passion shared
as we grow and heal together
finding comfort in ourselves.

Home

I have visited the child
I used to be.
I've held her close
while on my knees.

I felt her pain
as I knelt,
and in the safety of a hug
our tears made us melt.

You're safe with me.
There's nothing to fear.
I'm here for you
and I'll always care.

As we huddled close
in a heart-shared love,
we both were healed
from a power above.

My inner child
need no longer roam,
for here with me
she's found her home.

We Are the Teachers

The face of God
is on every child.
Divinity sparkles
in their eyes.
The smell of heaven
lingers in their skin
and nothing but love
pours from within.

As we cradle
these angels from above,
they teach us how
to give true love.
In their coos and smiles
we'll melt away,
and for a moment in time
God will guide the way.

They know
nothing of fear,
and hate can't be viewed.
They see
all skin colors
as beautiful hues.
The change in that scope
will come from you.

Let us be careful
of all that we teach.
Our actions dictate
everything they believe.
Their views are being molded
from our point of view:
angels or monsters,
it's all up to you.

The Learning Curve

Being a parent has given me tools
that I could never have learned in school
to combat stress
while being at my best.

School never taught me patience
since classrooms were for obedience,
but waiting for a tantrum to break
shows you exactly what is at stake.

They never taught me how to forgive
or even how just to live,
but tiny arms where they belong
makes my heart twice as strong.

As our children grow,
it's hard to know
where trouble lies
to cause their cries.

A parent's job is never done
with love so deep, it's next to none
and hugs so warm
they can calm the storm.

Of course, there are tears
that can exploit your cares
But they grow so fast
you just wish it would last.

I've mastered skills I need to cope
while always holding on to hope.
I've walked through darkness to the light,
and that is why I shine so bright.

The Story Ends

Oh let us dance another day!
I love it when I feel your sway.
The night is young
and our fever still burns;
every moment with you
our passion yearns.

As memories glitter in our eyes
the hands of time won't pass us by.
We're older now,
but still in love
as we dance together
fitting like a glove.

Hear the music of our heart
written for us at the very start.
It captures every moment spent
gazing together in eternity
as we can close our eyes
and drift away into infinity.

At My End

Please celebrate me
at my funeral
knowing I lived the life
that was meant for me.

Remember me
in the fullness of existence
of who I was
living as I wanted to be.

Have visions in your memories
of what you shared with me
and I hope you know the gratitude
that it all brought to me.

Remember to celebrate
with joyful passion
for the life
I was lucky to lead.

As I fold into Divinity
no regrets or look-backs for me
just the pleasure that I existed
being all that I could be.

About the Author

Sandra Leon-Gonzalez is a visionary poet of Jamaican heritage whose work bridges the sacred echoes of ancestral wisdom with the transformative power of truth, love, and light. Her previous titles include *Hear Me Roar: Poetry and Art** (2019), *Life Through Poetry and Art: Revisited* (2020), *Now I See* (2021), and *Finding My Wings* (2023).

Now, in *As We Soar*, she reclaims her narrative with fierce grace, breaking generational stereotypes and illuminating a path toward collective healing and unity for society and for her own four children. Rooted in the legacies of history and reaching toward the future, her poetry invites readers to rediscover their oneness and imagine a world where justice, equality, and truth are not ideals, but lived realities. Through this journey, Sandra offers not just poetry, but a movement—one that honors the past, empowers the present, and inspires the future.